bathroom
essentials

MAGGIE STEVENSON

bathroom

essentials

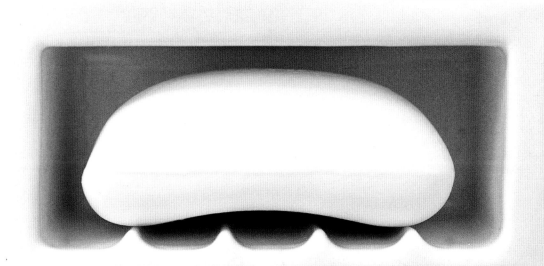

RYLAND
PETERS
& SMALL
LONDON NEW YORK

Designer Emilie Ekström
Senior editor Henrietta Heald
Picture research Emily Westlake
Production Deborah Wehner
Art director Gabriella Le Grazie
Publishing director Alison Starling

ISBN 1 84172 605 2

10 9 8 7 6 5 4 3 2 1

First published in the United Kingdom
in 2004 by Ryland Peters & Small
Kirkman House
12–14 Whitfield Street
London W1T 2RP
www.rylandpeters.com

Text copyright © Maggie Stevenson 2004
Design and photographs copyright
© Ryland Peters & Small 2004

All rights reserved. No part of this publication may be
reproduced, stored in a retrieval system or transmitted
in any form or by any means, electronic, mechanical,
photocopying, recording or otherwise, without written
permission from the publisher.

A CIP record for this book is available from the British Library.

Printed and bound in China.

contents

getting the

elements right

planning the space

The most efficient way to begin the planning process is to define the
role of your new bathroom. Will it be an en suite or family bathroom?
Is it likely to be used by more than one person at a time? Will any of
those using the bathroom be very young or old and infirm? Do you
want it to double as a dressing room? Do you like to bathe quickly or
in a leisurely way? Do you need storage only for toiletries or for towels
and cleaning products as well? Think about style, too. Do you favour
a contemporary or traditional look? Does the design need to integrate
with an adjoining room? The answers to these questions and others
like them will help you to decide your priorities.

Above This narrow corridor of a bathroom relies on glass, mirror and dramatic lighting to push back its boundaries. The working area is defined by its pale limestone wall and floor, and clear glass partitions separate the zones of activity.

Left A custom-made shower makes clever use of a confined space in this tiny internal bathroom. The curved shape eliminates the need for a shower door and its glass brick construction allows light to enter from an adjoining room.

Opposite, left and right This long, narrow bathroom has been made into a visually squarer, more comfortable space by fitting a shower cubicle across one end wall and building the bath into a raised platform at the other. Light emanating from above and below the wall behind the basin focuses attention at the centre of the room and adds to the impression of greater width.

The basic fixtures for a conventional bathroom are a basin, lavatory and bath, but there are many variations, and your choice will depend on the style you want, your budget and the size of your room. In a small bathroom the tub could be exchanged for a shower enclosure to save space – or, for a feeling of openness, the room could be designed as a fully waterproofed wet-room. If you want both a bath and shower, the choice is between separate fittings or an overbath shower. In some countries, every well-appointed bathroom contains a bidet, while in others it is an optional extra. Generally, top-quality fittings with designer labels are expensive, but there are plenty of good-looking alternatives in affordable ranges.

To see whether your fixtures will fit into the available space, draw a scale floor plan of the room and elevations of each wall on graph paper, then cut out cardboard shapes representing the fixtures to the same scale (manufacturers' brochures give exact sizes). On the floor plan and elevations, mark all permanent features such as windows and doorways, and place the cutouts on the plan, moving them around to find a feasible layout. Baths need a strip at least 90cm (36in) wide beside them to allow bathers to step out and dry themselves; showers need a space 70cm (28in) wide. Basins require 70cm (28in) in front and 20cm (8in) at each side; the lavatory and bidet need 60cm (24in) in front and 20cm (8in) at the sides. In a room used by one person at a time, access areas can be overlapped slightly, but bathrooms used by two or more people at once need extra space. While arranging the fixtures, refer to the elevations to identify any conflict with doors, windows or radiators. Doors can be re-hung or moved and radiators moved or replaced by underfloor heating to accommodate awkward layouts.

- Spend time getting your plans right. **Even small changes** like installing a shaver socket or an extractor fan **will be disruptive** if they are made later.

- Bathroom **fittings come in many shapes and sizes**; if you are planning a small or awkwardly shaped room, look at as many brochures as you can.

- If you want a chair, cabinet or other freestanding furniture in the room, allow for it **at the planning stage**.

- Pipework collects dirt and looks unsightly so **hide it behind boxed skirting boards**, false walls or some other form of ducting.

Above and left Open shelves and a console vanity unit leave the floor area in this bathroom uncluttered and easy to clean.
Opposite, above Designed for busy mornings, this compact shower room has a long basin that two can use at the same time. A flanking wall screens an open shower enclosure from the door.
Opposite, below A false wall constructed along one side of the bathroom neatly conceals the cistern for a back-to-the-wall lavatory and the plumbing for a shower.

Above Thick tinted glass forms a sleek countertop with integral circular bowls. Super stylish, it is also practical, with no joints where dirt and limescale can lodge.

Right and opposite, left Visually as well as physically weighty, the grey-brown mussel limestone covering most of the surfaces in this room is offset by expanses of white. On the horizontal, the stone is polished to show off the subtleties of its colour and texture, but on the vertical planes it is has been given narrow, regular grooves for textural and tonal contrast.

Opposite, right This superior form of duck boarding surrounding a sunken bath lets water drain through it.

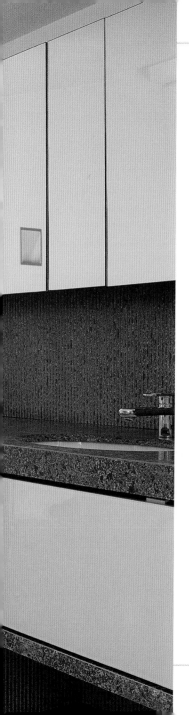

surfaces, flooring & lighting

The floor and walls form the background against which fixtures, furniture and accessories are seen. Since they make up such a large part of the picture, the materials covering them have a major influence on the style of a room; similar or complementary materials are likely to be used for the countertops, bath surround and other hardworking surfaces. Bathrooms require two distinct types of lighting: general all-over illumination and task lighting.

The ideal flooring for a conventional bathroom is water-tolerant, easy to clean, slip-resistant and warm to the touch. Vinyl, rubber and cork possess all these qualities but tile, stone, glass, wood and even carpet are suitable floor coverings provided they are chosen and used with care. Hard materials such as tile, stone and glass are often used in modern settings, but they are cold and potentially slippery when wet.

Wood and carpet may be the least water-tolerant materials, but they are comfortable to walk on and look luxurious. Unless you choose the kind specifically designed for bathrooms, laminated wood flooring may swell and distort in a damp environment, and solid timber requires careful sealing to protect against splinters and watermarks. Duck boarding and painted floorboards remain comparatively unscathed by water and can safely be used in adult bathrooms where the floor does not get too wet.

The range of wall treatments suitable for bathrooms is almost limitless provided the wet areas are properly protected. Continuous surfaces are often chosen for a contemporary scheme to give a sophisticated, seamless look, and for small spaces which appear all the more cramped if the walls are fragmented into a patchwork of textures and colours. Materials suitable for creating this all-over look include ceramic or glass tiles and mosaic and natural and synthetic stone, all of which are comparatively expensive but long-lasting,

Above Terracotta, hardwood, rubber and porcelain are all suitable flooring materials for wet areas and make strong foundations for specific bathroom styles. Terracotta tiles have a robust look and natural colour that warms country bathrooms; slatted timber is now the first choice for a smart urban setting; resilient, colourful rubber is a practical choice for a family bathroom; while porcelain offers a variety of size, shape and colour on a grand scale.
Opposite, right Random mosaic, corrugated PVC roofing and sheet vinyl flooring are inexpensive surface elements that combine harmoniously to create a practical and colourful bathroom.

Left Softwood is not generally recommended for bathroom flooring but exposed floorboards, naturally ventilated from beneath and painted to provide some protection from moisture, are serviceable and have a certain rustic charm. A cotton runner placed alongside the bath gives further protection from water where it is most needed, and is a soft surface to step onto.

waterproof and easy to clean. In traditional bathrooms and lower-budget installations, paint and wallpaper are decorative options for all walls other than those in the shower enclosure; if a uniform look is required, surfaces immediately around the bath and basin can be protected with clear glass or acrylic panels or plain matching tiles.

Wood panelling is an option for the walls of both traditional and modern bathrooms. In the bathrooms of period or country homes, painted tongue-and-groove wainscoting or fielded panelling covering the lower part of the wall may be continued around the room; they will withstand normal levels of bathroom moisture though not the direct spray of a

Above Drawn from nature, the floor in this bathroom is made from beach pebbles set in concrete, while the wall is clad with the pale, blond stems of bamboo.
Left Inexpensive plywood tiles take on a glamorous look when laid diamond fashion and studded with 'key-stones' of black-stained ply. Lacquer applied in several layers not only protects the wood from moisture but enhances its golden tones and gives it a satin sheen.

Below The tough industrial aesthetic of concrete is an interesting and unexpected contrast to sleek, domesticated materials such as lacquer and mirror glass. Custom-fabricated, it must be sealed before use.

Right Dark, handsome and expensive, iroko wood panelling remains unblemished by water. Lightly oiled to maintain its rich colour, the timber gives the room a sense of luxury and permanence.

Far right Porcelain tiles, whose colour and texture recall polished limestone, form a waterproof panel that can be distinguished from the wall only by its reflectivity. The mosaic bath panel adds further surface interest but allows no colour to intrude on this neutral scheme.

shower. Natural or oiled hardwood, such as iroko or merbau, is the modern alternative. Dark tropical timbers resist water to a degree, but will fade if not regularly oiled.

Smooth, pannelled surfaces are easier to clean than tiles or mosaic, which eventually accumulate grime in their grouted joints. The most popular of these are limestone, marble, granite, Corian and glass; in urban homes, industrial materials like concrete and sheet metals may be added to the list. All of these are hard-wearing, but extra care must be taken with limestone and marble which can be marked by acidic cleaners and cosmetics and badly damaged by cleaners that contain limescale remover.

As in other rooms in the home, the best general light in a bathroom is provided by daylight. In most bathrooms, you can maximize this by keeping window treatments simple, but in windowless internal bathrooms more radical measures will be necessary, such as replacing sections of the wall with glass bricks or obscured glass panels to allow light from an adjoining room to pass through.

After dark and on grey, wintry days, a central ceiling light, downlights recessed into the ceiling or wall fittings give even all-over light, leaving no gloomy spots in the room.

Bathroom task lighting – for activities such as shaving and applying make-up – centres on the mirror and should be directed so that it shines on your face. A pair of lights placed at the sides of the mirror will give a clear, virtually shadow-free light; the light sources may either be separate wall-mounted fittings or incorporated into the mirror itself.

Above A curve of obscured glass separates a shower area from a living space. Its frosted finish diffuses, and maximizes, the light passing through.
Left This dark, concrete-lined shower enclosure is studded at regular intervals with pale circular tiles that reflect light from the overhead fitting.
Right Light wood panelling gives a small bathroom a sophisticated look, and a large, unframed mirror increases the sense of space.
Opposite, above right A combination of hardwood decking and white mosaic tiles provides safe, moisture-resistant surfaces around a sunken bath.
Opposite, below right Loose-laid beach pebbles interspersed with uplighters form a natural border for a timber boardwalk floor.

- Stone is **a wonderful all-purpose surfacing material**, but in bathrooms it must be sealed.

- Industrial surfaces such as sheet metal, concrete and rubber create **an urban look**.

- Glass and mirror introduce glamour and **a sense of light and space**.

- Basins set into countertops are practical as well as good-looking; they can be made from **natural or synthetic stone, steel or glass**.

- Floor lights, spot lights and **concealing lights** add drama to a lighting scheme.

- For safety, all light fittings should be **purpose-made for bathroom use**.

fixtures & appliances

There are fixtures to suit every kind of bathroom. To pick your way through the bathroom maze, first identify your priorities and your personal style. Make a wish list of your ideal fittings, then whittle it down according to your budget, lifestyle and the space available. If you don't know what style you want, gather bathroom brochures, books and magazines and mark the pictures that appeal – you'll soon see if you lean towards modern or traditional shapes.

Above A mixer tap set into the marble top of a low partition wall at the foot of a bath projects into the tub to a lesser degree than it would do if it were wall- or rim-mounted, allowing for more comfortable bathing in a smaller than standard-size bathtub.

Right This custom-made glass basin – cantilevered from the wall with no visible means of support – is designed for washing under running water. Slim, shallow and with a backward-sloping base, it is long enough for two people to use at the same time, but it has a single plugless waste, so there is no possibility of water overflowing. Uncomplicated wall-mounted taps add to the minimalist effect.

Above and top Countertop basins come in various shapes to suit the style of room and the available space. Taps to fill them should be wall-mounted or extra-tall deck fittings.

Left A traditional fixed shower rose provides no choice of invigorating spray patterns – simply a heavy, drenching rain of water, with separate cross-head handles to control temperature and flow.

Popular bathtub materials include cast iron, enamelled steel, pressed acrylic and cast synthetics. Cast iron is heavy and stable with a lustrous porcelain enamelled finish; enamelled steel is lighter, and pressed acrylic lighter still. Cast synthetics mimic cast iron but are lighter and warm to the touch.

Most built-in baths are rectangular and available in a range of standard sizes, but corner baths and tapered baths are an option in small or awkwardly shaped rooms. Freestanding baths made from cast iron or cast synthetics come in modern oval shapes as well as the traditional roll-top form. While antique-style tubs stand on decorative legs, the modern ones have chunky wooden legs and rest on the floor, or on wooden or stone stands. To make the bath the main feature in the room, consider bespoke tubs made from stone, wood or stainless steel or an antique tub in ceramic or copper.

In Europe as well as America, a shower is now regarded as an essential piece of bathroom equipment, in addition to or instead of a bathtub. A separate shower enclosure is the ideal, but if space is tight, an overbath shower is a practical

Above The sprays from these twin showerheads overlap to give an even coverage within the large, rectangular shower enclosure. The exposed pipework supplying them is so neatly stapled along the ceiling that it makes minimal impact on the décor.

Right Although the bathtub is similar in shape to a comfortable Victorian roll-top bath, instead of having decorative cast-iron legs, this contemporary copy rests on angular limestone cradles, giving it a cleaner, more streamlined look that is more appropriate in a modern bathroom.

alternative. Shower enclosures consist of a shower tray and a waterproof surround. Usually, the shower tray is made from steel or a rigid synthetic material. The surround can be simply an alcove tiled or faced with stone or some other waterproof material, an enclosure formed by two glass or acrylic panels or a self-contained shower cubicle. The door may be hinged, but, if space is restricted, choose bi-fold, sliding or pivoting doors that open without encroaching on the room.

The fittings that deliver the shower spray draw on stored hot water or heat the water as required. Showers that use stored

Top, left to right Supataps with the handle and spout made as a single unit have a retro charm. A shower head with tiny projections directs the water in fine jets to give an invigorating spray. A modern freestanding bath is filled from a simple chrome spout rising from the floor and curving smoothly over the rim.

Above, left to right The combination of a fixed wide shower rose and a hand-held shower allows a choice between a relaxing overhead drench or targeted showering. Separate controls for temperature and flow allow you to establish your ideal setting. A three-hole mixer tap has separate controls for hot and cold water.

water offer the greatest choice of fittings, including fixed-head and hand-held sprays. More powerful showers that incorporate body sprays, foot sprays and deluge sprays may need a pump to increase water pressure.

Washbasins are many and varied. The choice is between a pedestal basin which rests on a ceramic column that hides the pipework, a cantilevered wall-mounted basin, a vanity basin mounted under or integrated into a countertop, a console basin that rests on or is built into a decorative stand, and a countertop basin, rectangular, oval or round, which stands on a shelf or tabletop. Most basins are made from glazed ceramic but other materials such as glass, stone, cast synthetics, stainless steel and wood are becoming more widely available.

Lavatories and bidets are floor-standing or wall-mounted. Ceramic is the most prevalent material for these fixtures, although stainless steel is sometimes preferred for bathrooms with an industrial aesthetic.

Taps are available in a wide range of traditional, classic and contemporary designs to match the baths and basins they fill. Finishes include chrome, nickel, gold and various antique effects and the most popular configurations are separate hot and cold pillar taps, three-hole mixers with handles to control hot and cold water and a separate spout and the monobloc or single lever mixer tap which controls the temperature and flow of the water.

Left The cistern and pipework for this wall-mounted bidet and lavatory are hidden in ducting, and the fixtures are suspended clear of the floor, so there are no awkward corners where dust and dirt can collect.
Below A valve-operated flush works efficiently and saves space but is not approved by every water authority.
Right This wide, shallow basin is a practical shape for washing and shaving.

- Before you buy a large bath made from **cast iron, stone or timber**, check that the floor will bear the combined weight of the tub and water.

- If you need extra storage, choose **a vanity basin with cupboard space below**. These can be made in contemporary and traditional styles.

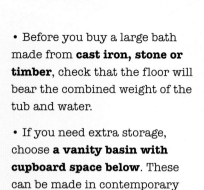

- In a small bathroom, **a shower cubicle with a sliding or folding door** will open without colliding with other fittings.

- Unless it will be used just for hand rinsing, buy the **largest bathroom basin** you can accommodate. It will contain splashes and allow for more **energetic washing**.

storage, furniture & accessories

A well-ordered bathroom is more conducive to relaxing, bathing and grooming than one that is littered with half-used shampoo bottles and damp towels. Good storage will bring the clutter under control. Built-in cupboards and vanity units generally provide bathroom storage, but there are situations where freestanding cabinets, rails, racks and containers are a useful addition or a practical alternative.

Left and above Glass shelves make good use of a space formerly occupied by a fireplace and its chimney. By day, the shelves' transparency contributes to the room's open, airy atmosphere, and at night, lights recessed into the top of the alcove beam through all the shelves, making a glowing display of the objects on them.
Opposite The bank of birchwood cabinets lining one side of this bathroom has twin washbasins mounted under its thick carrara marble countertop along with a series of cupboards and drawers. Raising the unit on short chrome legs makes the floor area seem larger and the unit itself less bulky.

Bathroom storage should combine open shelves or glazed cabinets for display and closed storage for those items you would prefer to hide. In bathrooms where space or budget is limited, the traditional bathroom cabinet mounted on the wall above the basin provides basic storage for essentials.

Floor-standing cabinets, trolleys and shelf units are a useful addition to most unfitted bathrooms. Cabinets are generally low and square, with a cupboard, drawers or a combination of the two. Storage trolleys are designed for manoeuvrability and may be fitted with brakes so they can be parked wherever they are needed. These mobile units range in style from mesh or polished metal trolleys to contemporary wooden designs and rustic painted cupboards.

Freestanding shelf units are efficient space savers. Like cabinets, they come in many materials. Glass shelves must be made from special toughened glass and have polished edges; they are ideal for small spaces since they allow light to pass through. Painted shelves are practical and easy to refresh with a new coat of paint when they begin to look shabby. Wire mesh is well suited to shelves, but the mesh will not contain spilt liquids. Although wooden shelves intended for bathroom use will be protected with a durable finish, furniture that has been designed for other rooms may not be so resistant to bathroom products. Even in the smallest bathroom, space can be found to

This page Built-in and close-fitting cupboards and drawers turn unused spaces into storage. Stained plywood drawers fill the space under a concrete vanity unit; silky, pale birch cupboards and drawers are recessed into the wall; while a huge wardrobe with imposing panelled oak doors slots neatly into an alcove.

Opposite Simple and relatively inexpensive ideas can solve specific storage problems. An antique shelf fitted high on the wall at the foot end of the tub holds fresh towels within easy reach of the person using the overbath shower. A wicker hamper stores towels and spare lavatory paper, and a purpose-made wall- or door-mounted rack keeps magazines tidy.

hang wall shelves. Ready-made units are simply screwed to the wall but cut-to-size shelves will fit any available space.

Towel rails keep towels tidy and allow them to air after use. Unheated towel rails are made of wood, plastic or metal and can be wall-mounted or floor-standing. The wall-mounted types take the form of a ring or a single or double straight rail supported on brackets in a design to match other wall-mounted bathroom accessories. Rings for hand towels are placed beside a basin or bidet, but straight rails are large enough to hold a bath towel. Floor-standing rails usually have more than one rail and allow several towels to air at once.

Right Invaluable in a bathroom where shelf space is limited, this slim vertical rail, reaching from floor to ceiling, supports towel rails, tooth mug and a swing-arm magnifying mirror that is adjustable to various levels.

Below left Every shower enclosure needs somewhere to rest the soap or sponge, and this minimal stainless-steel holder is in keeping with the urban style of its concrete and mosaic surroundings.

Below right An alcove, recessed into the wall at eye level and tiled with the same mosaic, is roomy enough to hold a selection of hair-care and shower preparations.

Individual wall-mounted holders for soaps, sponges, shaving equipment, toothbrushes and toilet rolls can be fixed where they are needed. In the shower, corner-fitting shelves and tiered sets of wire baskets hold shower gel and shampoos within easy reach.

Most wall-mounted racks and holders are screwed to the wall, but in areas with tiled or glass walls, fittings that are attached by suction pads are easier to install.

Bath racks that rest like a bridge across the bathtub hold all the necessary equipment for bathing, and some luxurious models have integral book rests, candle holders or a shaving mirror.

Left Small, cylindrical pegs offer discreet hanging space for towels, bathrobes and toilet bags. The serpentine tubular heated towel rail has hinged fixings, allowing it to fold flat against the wall or swing out to hold thick towels or warm the room more quickly. **Far left** Heated towel rails with wider spaces between groups of rails let air circulate freely, allowing towels to dry more quickly. **Below** Laundry baskets do not have to be made of wicker – any moisture-resistant, washable material will do. If you choose a design such as this plywood bin that may also be used as a seat, check before you buy that it is sturdy enough for the purpose.

A laundry basket helps to keep the room tidy. Towels and clothes can be dropped into it the moment they are discarded. Some laundry bins are lined with a fabric bag which can be detached, allowing the laundry to be carried straight to the washing machine.

In most bathrooms, furnishings are limited to the essentials, but if you add a chair the atmosphere immediately becomes more relaxed and inviting. In a large, well-ventilated bathroom decorated in traditional or country style, an upholstered armchair brings comfort and a touch of luxury, but in a smaller space, light, moisture-resistant wicker or loom is a better choice. In a modern bathroom, a

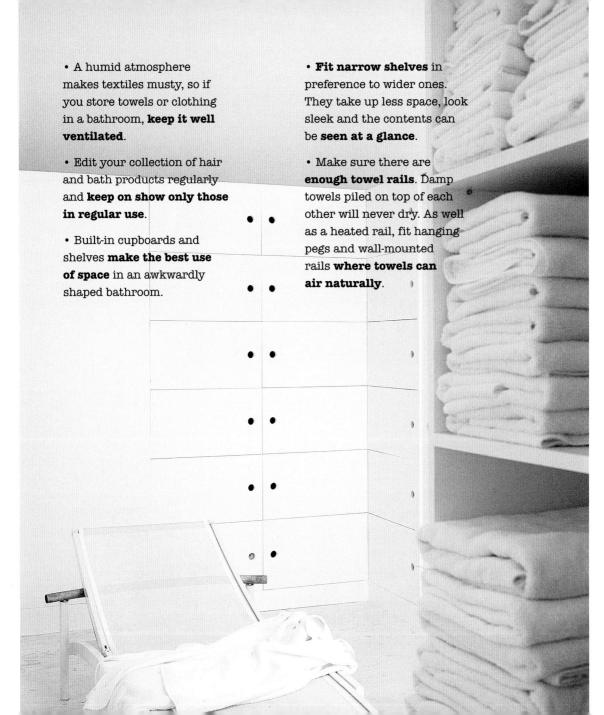

• A humid atmosphere makes textiles musty, so if you store towels or clothing in a bathroom, **keep it well ventilated**.

• Edit your collection of hair and bath products regularly and **keep on show only those in regular use**.

• Built-in cupboards and shelves **make the best use of space** in an awkwardly shaped bathroom.

• **Fit narrow shelves** in preference to wider ones. They take up less space, look sleek and the contents can be **seen at a glance**.

• Make sure there are **enough towel rails**. Damp towels piled on top of each other will never dry. As well as a heated rail, fit hanging pegs and wall-mounted rails **where towels can air naturally**.

shapely plastic chair produced by one of the modern makers will be impervious to water and contribute to the contemporary style. Bathrooms too small for a chair generally have room for a stool or folding café chair.

The extra surfaces and storage provided by a small table, chest of drawers or small cupboard are not, strictly speaking, essential in a bathroom, but if you are aiming for a softer, more lived-in look than pared-down functionalism, they are a worthwhile addition.

A small table or cabinet drawn alongside the tub makes a suitable place to put your book, a drink and the radio while you indulge in a relaxing bath, and a chest of drawers with a mirror hung above it will serve as an attractive dressing table.

Above Magnifying mirrors are needed for tasks that require a close-up view; one that tilts and swivels is the most versatile.

Above left Wall-mounted shelves and holders are necessary adjuncts to a traditional pedestal basin that has limited space for essentials.

Left A bamboo stool is useful as a seat or surface and can withstand a moist atmosphere.

Far left The narrow shelf that runs the length of this bathroom is a valuable storage space; to avoid a cluttered effect, the items on it are arranged in neat groups.

Opposite Designed like a locker room, the walls of this dressing room are lined with cupboards of various sizes and open shelves.

putting it

together

Right A semi-sunken bath screened by a low, toughened-glass panel barely impacts on the space in this small bathroom. Wall-mounted fittings let light flow uninterrupted around the room.

Below Unusually for a shower enclosure, the walls, rendered with the waterproof plaster used to line swimming pools, are slightly gritty to the touch, but the slate floor and reinforced-glass shelves offer a smooth contrast.

contemporary

The bathroom lends itself well to contemporary style. Its cool, smooth surfaces, sculptural fittings, and highly engineered plumbing combine to create a capsule environment of calm and order that is, for many of us, impossible to maintain with any success elsewhere in the home.

Above Hard surfacing need not mean a cold and spartan look. A large bath and even larger shower area lined with creamy limestone and frosted glass, carefully lit to dramatic effect, create a warm and indulgent bathroom.

Left Colour in a monochromatic scheme or a familiar material used in an unusual way make an essentially formal design memorable. Here, the unexpected element is the countertop. Made from blue glass with twin integral washbasins, the surface is raised above a bank of plain, white cabinets, leaving a shelf between the two. Light passing through the tinted glass illuminates the space beneath with an eerie glow.

The pioneers of the contemporary look were in search of simplicity to counter the complexity of modern life – and they turned to natural materials, naked and unadorned, to create it. Their theory worked. A visually quiet space undoubtedly has restorative powers, and although at first the materials and fittings needed to create it were expensive and readily available only to architects and designers, they have now come within reach of a wider public.

Surfaces that have the right aesthetic credentials for this look include natural materials such as hardwood and stone, and products such as brick, metal and concrete that have been used in the building industry for generations but were rarely visible in interiors. Add to these glass and modern man-made surfacing materials such as Corian and Lucite and the scope of contemporary style broadens to encompass a wide range of decorating options.

One of the most recent developments in contemporary bathrooms is the bolder use of colour. Previously, colour was limited to a natural palette based on the raw materials used for the décor, but gradually mosaic tiles – a cheaper surfacing

Left Metallic wallpapers inject light and drama into a dark bathroom; this one, depicting iconic film stars, adds a touch of glamour.
Above left Hanging a single vibrant picture can send shockwaves through the polite elegance of a dark monochromatic scheme.
Far left Many modern bathrooms incorporate natural materials, but those that include man-made surfaces are more colourful and vigorous. The colour in this shower room is at its most conspicuous in the transparent acrylic basin surround and shower screen.

material than stone or timber and available in shimmering, watery pastels that complement the natural tones – were added to give gentle contrast. More intense colours have followed in the form of synthetic surfaces and glass tiles, the latter being available in slip-resistant varieties for floors as well as walls.

Finding sanitary fittings, taps and showers in contemporary style has never been easier. The seminal designs of well-known architects and industrial designers will always be the purists' first choice, but the mass-market ranges they have inspired and the functional no-frills fittings produced for the building trade make acceptable and affordable substitutes. Large, focal-point baths made from stone, resin or timber, countertop basins in ceramic, glass, steel or stone, deceptively simple taps and wall-mounted lavatories and bidets all contribute to the modern look.

Above The design of some modern bathrooms has become formulaic with the same materials and fittings appearing in different permutations. A uniquely personal effect that is no less current in style is achieved by combining materials in unusual partnerships. This bathroom mixes wood veneer, aluminium, glass and ceramic tiles in an unusually muscular scheme.
Left Slate cut into thin tiles is suitable for both walls and floors, but because the stone is a dense, dark grey, rooms where it is used extensively must be brightly lit.

simplicity and clean lines . . .

If you need to partition the space in a bathroom, use **glass bricks or panels** – clear or frosted – to allow **light to flood through**.

Remember that **wood, stone and concrete** all need to be sealed to make them water-resistant.

Introduce colour in the form of mosaic, glass tiles or synthetic **surfacing materials**.

Sanitary fittings, taps and showers in **simple shapes** and wall-mounted lavatories with concealed cisterns all add to **the streamlined look**.

If you have the budget, a custom-made **countertop with an integral washbasin** is a sophisticated alternative to undermounted bowls.

for modern elegance

country

Luxury and indulgence are present in the typical country-style bathroom – but in the uncomplicated form of thick, laundry-roughened towels, lavender-scented bath water and a window with a green and pleasant view.

Above Antique fairs and sale rooms are the places to look for old bathroom fixtures such as this enamelled basin. Before you buy, check carefully for cracks and chips, which cannot be successfully repaired.

Right Painted wood panelling, a carpet on the floor and pictures on the wall give this bathroom a relaxed and homely air. The modern bath, raised on chunky turned wood feet and placed alongside a vintage washbasin, adapts well to its traditional surroundings.

Above Few modern basins are as pretty as this Victorian one with its floral transfer decoration. Modern reproductions are available, but they never accurately replicate the deep, inky, indigo blue that makes the original patterns unique.

Left The terrazzo floor, cast-iron bath and tiled walls have given good service for more than five decades. The décor still looks fresh and the addition of a pleated blind at the window and an industrial-style enamelled light fitting give it a cared-for look that does not detract from its retro charm.

Many bathrooms in traditional country homes have been converted from spare bedrooms, and often have enough space to allow a more imaginative layout than is possible in a modern bathroom. If they are retained, built-in cupboards, window seats, alcoves and other features of the original room add character. A smaller bathroom, built as an extension or squeezed into space partitioned from a large bedroom or landing, will need clever decoration to give it style.

Suitable reclaimed and reproduction fittings come in a variety of shapes, but if your aim is to create a bathroom that is visually embedded in its surroundings, choose only those that match the status of the building. Victorian or Edwardian sanitaryware, perhaps

Left and far left Typical elements of country style include the stripped-pine door, traditional shower, fabric curtain and chunky wooden shelf.
Below Small details have a big impact and these old enamel pots labelled for 'soap' and 'sand' reinforce the traditional look.
Opposite, top Old and new come together in this vanity stand made by plumbing a modern basin into a painted antique chest.
Opposite, below left A sauna is part of everyday life in northern Europe, but still regarded as a luxury further south. As the temperature rises, the wood of the walls and benches fills the air with its resinous scent.
Opposite, below right A porcelain-handled spray distinguishes this traditional bath/shower mixer.

with floral decoration, is an appropriate choice for larger country houses, while in a modest country cottage simple fixtures in designs from the 1920s or 1930s would be more suitable. Barns and other converted farm buildings are, by definition, modern, but fixtures in plain shapes are a good match for their pared-down character.

The bath is the dominant feature of a country bathroom. A roll-top tub has the right vintage look and is impressive enough to stand in the centre of a large bathroom. In a smaller space, a standard bath placed along a wall and boxed in with tongue-and-groove panelling has a suitably nostalgic feel.

Ceramic tiles and painted wood are good choices for wall and floor coverings in a traditional setting. Plain white or cream rectangular wall tiles hung brick-fashion have a retro look, but square tiles taken to eye level and edged with a narrow black border or a patchwork of patterned Victorian tiles would also work well. Tiles and timber are also ideal for flooring. For a traditional look, create a chequered effect with black and white tiles or scrub the floorboards and leave them bare.

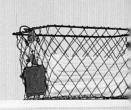

a new life for old things and . . .

Choose fittings for **visual appeal**. A console washbasin with decorative **ceramic or metal legs** is a pretty alternative to an urban vanity unit.

Reproduction baths and basins take on **an authentic look** when fitted with antique taps.

Ceramic jugs, **enamel mugs** and other finds from bric-a-brac stalls make bathroom accessories with **the right period charm**.

Pale, printed cotton curtains, a snowy linen blind or white-painted shutters all **filter the light** and give privacy.

If you need more storage, **search sale rooms or antique fairs** for cupboards or chests of drawers.

a breath of country air

Left and opposite The space to make an en suite bathroom must sometimes be stolen from the bedroom itself. Less expensive than building a solid wall between the two zones, frosted-glass panels screening the washbasin and overbath shower areas give privacy where it is needed and contain the wet areas. The use of translucent materials and an open-plan layout means that the bathing area does not feel cramped nor the bedroom too much reduced.

Below Building a shower under the roof slope in a loft conversion makes sense as long as there is full head height in the place where the person using it will be standing. A larger floor area – however low the ceiling at the furthest point – will give a feeling of space within the enclosure.

small bathrooms

Lack of space is so common in a bathroom that it barely registers as a design challenge, but now that bathing is an act of self-indulgence as much as a daily routine, the room must reflect its dual role. A well-planned layout, careful use of colour and some ingenious design tricks will stretch the limits of a compact room, making it seem comfortable but never cramped.

A mixture of pale colours, clear glass and reflective surfaces can create an illusion of space in a small bathroom. Moreover, improved plumbing and specially designed fixtures mean there is no reason why compactness should preclude efficiency and elegance. The en suite bathroom in a good hotel demonstrates how successful a small bathroom can be. Rarely larger than is absolutely necessary, it contains all the essentials, yet still manages to convey a sense of luxury through its streamlined layout and use of top-quality fittings and surfaces. The domestic bathroom differs from this only in its need to include adequate storage.

In a compact space, cupboards and drawers are preferable to open shelves because they allow you to reduce the amount of clutter on view and make good use of otherwise dead areas under the basin, in alcoves and behind the panelling that conceals cisterns and pipework and encloses the bath.

The way fittings are arranged within a room affects how spacious it seems. As well as making a floor plan, it is worth drawing an elevation of each wall so you can take the height and bulk of the fixtures into account as well as the ground space they occupy. It is tempting to find room for all the fixtures on your wish list but sometimes the layout works better, and the room feels more open, if you compromise by having an over-bath shower instead of a separate shower

Below Hinged doors require space to open, but in this shower room sliding doors have been fitted to the cabinets as well as to the entrance, allowing every little bit of floor space to be put to work.

Opposite, below Barely larger than an average cloakroom, this tiny shower room relies on good lighting and the pale colours of natural limestone to enhance its modest dimensions. A clear, frameless partition divides the space without visually compartmentalizing it.

Opposite, above Sometimes, because it is usually seen in the context of a larger room, a single imposing piece of furniture creates the illusion of space. Here, a large mirror, a glazed door and white walls balance the dark wooden vanity unit and ensure that it does not dominate completely.

enclosure or install a large shower instead of a tub. A less crowded room will feel relaxed, look better and be more convenient to use.

Visual devices to make a small room seem bigger include allowing light to flow through the space by choosing a frameless shower enclosure glazed with clear toughened glass – or even abandoning enclosures and partitions altogether in favour of a wet-room where all surfaces are waterproofed. Wall-mounted fittings make the floor area appear larger, and cabinets or vanity units that are raised on legs have a less bulky look. Even oddly shaped rooms can be made to feel more comfortable. For example, in a tall, narrow space, the perceived height can be reduced by tiling the walls to a level that stops short of the ceiling.

To reduce the apparent length of a long, narrow room, the tub can be placed across its width at one end, and an open shower area across it at the other. Arranging the other fixtures along one wall between them will give an impression of space at the centre of the room, which can be accentuated by putting mirrors on opposite sides of the room and hanging a lamp centrally over the area.

One way to give a more streamlined look both inside and outside a bathroom is to replace hinged doors with sliding pocket doors. Unlike track-mounted doors, which side over the wall they open onto, pocket doors are fitted in double-thickness walls and, when open, disappear into the space between the leaves of the wall.

light plays a crucial part . . .

Ducting may reduce the size of the room slightly but it **hides pipework** and the lavatory cistern, giving a neat look, and **storage can be recessed into it**.

Try **decorating the room** entirely in a single colour or material. **Continuity** adds to a calm, relaxed atmosphere.

Cool, light colours such as **pale blue, lilac and aqua** seem to recede, making a room seem larger.

Make use of awkward spaces **in alcoves or under the eaves** for storage or activities that don't require **a full-height ceiling**.

in creating a sense of space

family-friendly

Families are never static, and in a household with young children the bathroom should be flexible enough to adapt as they grow. Get the basics right by providing efficient heating, waterproof surfaces and robust fittings that will stand up to the heavy wear they will inevitably receive, and respond to your children's developing tastes by changing the décor and accessories.

Above To prevent children locking themselves in the bathroom by accident, fit latches that can be opened from the outside.
Left An open-plan, en suite bathroom is a parents' sanctuary, but for children the chance to bathe in such a luxurious grown-up space is a special treat; a lockable door is essential if you want to keep this personal space private.
Right A few well-chosen accessories can alter the style of a plain white bathroom. A primary-coloured shower curtain and tooth mug will appeal to younger children and can easily be replaced as their tastes develop.

Very young children need help with every aspect of personal care from teeth-cleaning to using the lavatory, so bathrooms designed for families must have plenty of clear space to allow parent and child to move around easily. The bath in particular needs enough space for a parent to kneel or sit beside the tub to supervise bathing, read stories or just discuss the day before helping their child towel dry and put on their pyjamas.

When choosing fittings, opt for a bigger bath – preferably with taps and plug hole placed centrally – so two children can bathe at the same time. If there is room, fit twin basins; they will be invaluable when children start school and the whole family needs to leave home at the same time in the morning.

Walls, floors and other surfaces should be both safe and practical. Floors must be waterproof, slip-resistant and warm to the touch. Materials such as rubber, linoleum, cork and vinyl have the right characteristics and, unlike ceramic tiles, provide a relatively soft landing if accidents do happen.

Left Built-in storage alcoves keep bathtime necessities close at hand.
Below This translucent plastic shower curtain with pockets is used as an ever-changing gallery of family photographs.
Opposite, left A square bath, tailored to fit the space, with a ledge all round for toys and toiletries, is large enough to bathe two or three children at once.
Opposite, above right A wide shelf makes a useful changing area for a small baby, and open shelves offer easy-access storage.
Opposite, below right Twin basins save time in the morning rush hour, and mirrored cabinets recessed flush with the wall are less inviting to younger children.

Children tend to splash water around, and wall and surface materials that wipe down easily and won't be damaged by water are ideal. Tiles or special bathroom paints are the most tolerant wall treatments, while laminate, tile or stone surfaces for shelves and the tops of units are good-looking and robust.

Provide plenty of storage in the form of pegs to hold dressing gowns, laundry bags and towels, open shelves for things in frequent use such as toiletries, spare towels, baby-changing items and toys, and cupboards – some of them lockable – to keep potentially hazardous cleaning products, medicines and perfume sprays out of harm's way.

Try colour-coding toothbrushes, mugs and towels to remind children to use only their own personal kit and fit rails lower on the wall to encourage them to hang up towels. Allow early independence by providing sturdy, stable step stools to give easier access to the basin and lavatory.

thoughtful details help to make . . .

Make it **easy for children** to keep the bathroom tidy by fitting **pegs and rails** at a height they can easily reach.

To reduce the risk of falls choose **slip-resistant flooring,** mop up spilt liquids and keep the floor clear of toys, step-stools and **other obstacles**.

spaces fun for children

Choose a bright colour scheme. In case the décor outlasts your children's taste for **a primary palette**, introduce the colour in accessories and towels that can be **easily changed**.

Keep medicines and cleaners **under lock and key**.

Reduce the risk of scalding by opting for **a mixer instead of separate hot and cold taps**.

suppliers

Aqualisa Products
The Flyers Way
Westerham
Kent TN16 1DE
01959 563240
www.aqualisa.co.uk
High-quality showers.

Armitage Shanks
Armitage, Rugeley
Staffs WS15 4BT
01543 490253
www.armitage-shanks.co.uk
Comprehensive selection of
fixtures including whirlpool
and spa baths.

Aston Matthews
141–47 Essex Road
London N1 2SN
020 7226 7220
www.astonmatthews.co.uk
Traditional and modern
fixtures and fittings.

Bathstore.com
410–14 Upper Richmond Rd
London SW14 7JX
020 8870 8888
And stores nationwide.
www.bathstore.com
Everything for the
bathroom.

Bathroom City
Tyseley Industrial Estate
Birmingham B25 8ET
0121 753 0700
www.bathroomcity.co.uk
Bathroom superstore.

Bhs
252–58 Oxford Street
London W1N 9DC
020 7629 2011
Branches nationwide.
www.bhs.co.uk
Good-value lighting and
bathroom accessories.

Caradon Mira
Cromwell Road
Cheltenham
Gloucestershire GL52 5EP
01242 221221
High-quality showers.

Colourwash
165 Chamberlayne Road
London NW10 3NU
020 8459 8918
www.colourwash.co.uk
Contemporary bathroom
fittings and accessories.

CP Hart
Newnham Terrace
Hercules Road
London SE1 7DR
020 7902 1000
And branches.
Wide range of sanitaryware.

Czech & Speake
39c Jermyn Street
London SW1Y 6DN
020 8980 4567
www.czechspeake.com
Traditional-style fittings.

Fired Earth
Twyford Mill
Oxford Road, Adderbury
Banbury
Oxfordshire OX17 3HP
01295 814300
www.firedearth.com
Bathroom fittings and tiles
in traditional and modern
designs. Shops nationwide.

Habitat
196 Tottenham Court Road
London W1T 7LG
020 7631 3880 or
0645 334433 for branches
www.habitat.net
Good-value modern lighting
and bathroom accessories.

Heal's
196 Tottenham Court Road
London W1T 7LG
020 7636 1666 or
0645 334433 for branches
www.heals.co.uk
Storage and accessories.

The Holding Company
241–45 King's Road
London SW3 5EL
020 7352 1600
Mail order 020 8445 2888
www.theholdingcompany.
co.uk
Storage for small bathrooms.

Ideal Standard and Sottini
The Bathroom Works
National Avenue
Hull HU5 4HS
01482 499380
Bathrooms in all styles.

Ikea
255 North Circular Road
London NW13 0JQ
020 8208 5600 for
branches and catalogue
www.ikea.co.uk
Self-assembly units or
delivery and installation
available.

John Lewis
278–306 Oxford Street
London W1A 1EX
020 7629 7111
www.johnlewis.co.uk
Towels and stylish basics.

Majestic Shower Company
1 North Place
Edinburgh Way, Harlow
Essex CN20 2SL
01279 443644
www.majesticshowers.com
Glass tiles and frameless
shower enclosures.

Marks & Spencer
458 Oxford Street
London W1C 1AP
020 7935 7954
www.marksandspencer.com
Towels and accessories.

Nordic
Unit 5, Fairview Estate
Holland Road
Hurst Green, Oxted
Surrey RH8 9BZ
01882 716111
www.nordic.co.uk
Saunas, steam rooms,
showers, whirlpools.

Ocean
08770 2426283
www.oceanuk.com
Mail-order catalogue with
contemporary accessories.

Old Fashioned Bathrooms
The Foresters Hall
52 High Street
Debenham
Suffolk IP14 6QW
01728 860926
www.oldfashionedbathrooms.
co.uk
Victorian, Edwardian and
reproduction fixtures.

Samuel Heath & Sons
Leopold Street
Birmingham B12 0UJ
0800 0191 282
www.samuel-heath.com
High-quality taps and
bathroom accessories

Shires Bathrooms
Beckside Road, Bradford
West Yorks BD7 2JE
01274 521199
www.shires-bathrooms.co.uk
Modern and traditional
bathroom suites.

Triton
Newdagate Street, Nuneaton
Warwickshire CV11 4EU
01203 344441
www.tritonshowers.co.uk
Electric and power showers.

Vernon Tutbury
Silverdale
Newcastle-under-Lyme
Staffordshire ST5 6EL
01782 717175
www.qpinteriors.co.uk
Luxury bathroom suites.

Villeroy & Boch
267 Merton Road
London SW18 5JS
020 8871 4028
www.villeroy-boch.com
Stylish fittings and furniture.

Vola
Unit 12
Ampthill Business Park
Station Road, Ampthill
Bedfordshire MK45 2QW
01525 841155
www.vola.co.uk
Sleek modern designs,
including taps and fittings
by Arne Jacobsen.

Water Monopoly
16–18 Lonsdale Road
London NW6 6RD
020 7624 2636
www.watermonopoly.co.uk
Beautifully restored antique
and reproduction French
and English sanitaryware.

credits

Key: ph=photographer, a=above, b=below, r=right, l=left, c=centre.
All photography by Chris Everard unless otherwise stated.

Front jacket Jan Baldwin/Constanze von Unruh's house in London; **page 1** interior designer Alan Tanksley's own apartment in Manhattan; **2** ph Debi Treloar/Susan Cropper's family home in London, www.63hlg.com; **3** New York City apartment designed by Marino + Giolito; **4r** Simon Crookall's apartment in London designed by Urban Salon ; **5** ph Jan Baldwin/David Gill's house in London; **6–7** ph Henry Bourne/Dan and Claire Thorne's town house in Dorset designed by Sarah Featherstone; **8** both Fred Wadsworth's flat in London designed by Littman Goddard Hogarth; **9l** an apartment in Paris designed by Bruno Tanquerel; **9r** Simon Brignall & Christina Rosetti's loft apartment in London designed by David Mikhail Architects; **10l** a house in London designed by Carden & Cunietti; **10r** Andrew Wilson's house in London designed by Azman Owens; **11** both Vicente Wolf's home on Long Island; **12l** Monique Witt and Steven Rosenblum's apartment in New York, designed by Mullman Seidman Architects; **12–13 & 13c** ph Andrew Wood/a house near Antwerp designed by Claire Bataille and Paul ibens; **13r** Heidi Wish & Philip Wish's apartment in London designed by Moutarde & Heidi Wish; **14al** ph Ray Main/Client's residence, East Hampton, New York, designed by ZG DESIGN; **14ar** a house in London designed by Carden & Cunietti; **14bl** Andrew Wilson's apartment in London designed by Azman Owens; **14br** New York City apartment designed by Marino + Giolito; **15l** ph Andrew Wood/Roger Oates and Fay Morgan's house in Eastnor; **15r** ph Alan Williams/Richard Oyarzarbal's apartment in London designed by Urban Research Laboratory; **16l** John Minshaw's house in London designed by John Minshaw; **16r** Henry Bourne/Linda Trahair's house in Bath; **17l** Stephan Schulte's loft apartment in London; **17c** ph Andrew Wood/Roger and Suzy Black's apartment in London designed by Johnson Naylor; **17r** ph Andrew Wood/house in London designed by Bowles and Linares; **18l** an apartment in New York designed by David Deutsch & Sidnam Petrone Gartner Architects; **18r** One New Inn Square, a private dining room and home of chef David Vanderhook, enquiries 020 7729 3645; **19l** ph Ray Main/Jonathan Reed's apartment in London, lighting designed by Sally Storey, design director of John Cullen Lighting; **19ar** Michael Nathenson's house in London; **19br** Simon Brignall & Christina Rosetti's loft apartment in London designed by David Mikhail Architects; **20l** ph Jan Baldwin/Peter & Nicole Dawes' apartment, designed by Mullman Seidman Architects; **20r** a house in Hampstead, London designed by Orefelt Associates; **21l** an apartment in Paris designed by Bruno Tanquerel; **21ar** Jan Baldwin/Constanze von Unruh's house in London; **21br** architect Nigel Smith's apartment in London; **22a** Richard Hopkin's apartment in London designed by HM2; **22b** ph Jan Baldwin/art dealer Gul Coskun's apartment in London; **23al&bc** Heidi Wish & Philip Wish's apartment in London designed by Moutarde & Heidi Wish; **23ac** Hudson Street Loft designed by Moneo Brock Studio; **23ar** Freddie Daniells' apartment in London designed by Brookes Stacey Randall; **23bl** Suze Orman's apartment in New York designed by Patricia Seidman of Mullman Seidman Architects; **23br** ph Jan Baldwin/Christopher Leach's apartment in London; **24a** Richard Hopkin's apartment in London designed by HM2; **24b** New York City apartment designed by Marino + Giolito; **25** Pemper and Rabiner home in New York, designed by David Khouri of Comma; **26** designed by Mullman Seidman Architects; **27** both ph Alan Williams/Gail & Barry Stephens' house in London; **28a** Monique Witt and Steven Rosenblum's apartment in New York, designed by Mullman Seidman Architects; **28bl** Heidi Wish & Philip Wish's apartment in London designed by Moutarde & Heidi Wish; **28br** Michael Nathenson's house in London; **29al** a house in Paris designed by Bruno Tanquerel; **29ar** Suze Orman's apartment in New York designed by Patricia Seidman of Mullman Seidman Architects; **29b** Mark Kirkley & Harumi Kaijima's house in Sussex; **30a** Alison Thompson & Billy Paulett's house in London designed by Stephen Turvil Architects; **30bl** a house in London by Seth Stein; **30br** ph Debi Treloar/Ian Hogarth's family home; **30–31a** Richard Oyarzabal's apartment in London designed by Jeff Kirby of Urban Research Laboratory; **31a** a house in Hampstead, London designed by Orefelt Associates; **31b** Freddie Daniells' apartment in London designed by Brookes Stacey Randall; **32** ph Andrew Wood/ Johanne Riss' house in Brussels; **33al** New York City apartment designed by Marino + Giolito; **33ar** Vicente Wolf's home on Long Island; **33bl** Simon Brignall & Christina Rosetti's loft apartment in London designed by David Mikhail Architects; **33br** Paul Brazier & Diane Lever's house in London designed by Carden & Cunietti; **34–35** Calvin Tsao & Zack McKown's apartment in New York designed by Tsao & McKown; **36l** Stephan Schulte's loft apartment in London; **36r** Ian Chee of VX design & architecture; **37l** Monique Witt and Steven Rosenblum's apartment in New York, designed by Mullman Seidman Architects; **37r** Freddie Daniells' apartment in London designed by Brookes Stacey Randall; **38a** John Barman's Park Avenue Apartment; **38bl** ph Alan Williams/Hudson Street Loft designed by Moneo Brock Studio; **38br** Sera Hersham-Loftus' house in London; **39l** Gomez/ Murphy Loft, Hoxton, London designed by Urban Salon ; **39r** One New Inn Square, a private dining room and home of chef David Vanderhook, enquiries 020 7729 3645; **40al** a house in Hampstead, London designed by Orefelt Associates; **40bl** ph Debi Treloar/family home, Bankside, London; **40r** ph Debi Treloar/a house by Knott Architects in London; **41l** ph Andrew Wood/Johanne Riss' house in Brussels; **41c** ph James Morris/the Jackee' and Elgin Charles House in California's Hollywood Hills, designed by William R. Hefner AIA, interior design by Sandy Davidson Design; **41r** Hilton McConnico's house near Paris; **42l** ph Tom Leighton/lofts in the old centre of Amsterdam of Annette Brederode, painter & dealer/collector of antiques and 'brocante' and Aleid Röntgen-Brederode, landscape architect; **42r** ph Tom Leighton; **43l** ph Tom Leighton/ Roxanne Beis' home in Paris; **43r** Sera Hersham-Loftus' house in London; **44bl** a house in

Hampstead, London designed by Orefelt Associates; **44ar** Frazer Cunningham's house in London; **44br** a house in Paris designed by Bruno Tanquerel; **45a both** a house in London designed by Helen Ellery of The Plot London; **45b** ph Tom Leighton; **46al** a house in Paris designed by Bruno Tanquerel; **46bl** ph Tom Leighton; **46r, 47l & 47ar** ph Debi Treloar/Kristiina Ratia and Jeff Gocke's family home in Norwalk, Connecticut; **47br** Emma & Neil's house in London, walls painted by Garth Carter; **48 & 48–49** Alison Thompson & Billy Paulett's house in London designed by Stephen Turvil Architects; **49b** ph Jan Baldwin/a house in New York designed by Brendan Coburn and Joseph Smith from Coburn Architecture; **50l** a house in Hampstead, London designed by Orefelt Associates; **50r** an apartment in New York, designed by Mullman Seidman Architects; **51** Pemper and Rabiner home in New York, designed by David Khouri of Comma; **52** main Central Park West Residence, New York City designed by Bruce Bierman Design; **52 inset** an apartment in New York, designed by Mullman Seidman Architects; **52–53** Fifth Avenue Residence, New York City designed by Bruce Bierman Design;

53bl Yuen-Wei Chew's apartment in London designed by Paul Daly Design Studio; **53ar&br** Ben Atfield's house in London; **54l** ph Debi Treloar/ Paul Balland and Jane Wadham of jwflowers.com's family home in London; **54r** Monique Witt and Steven Rosenblum's apartment in New York, designed by Mullman Seidman Architects; **55** ph Debi Treloar/Victoria Andreae's house in London; **56l** ph Debi Treloar/a house by Knott Architects in London; **56ar** ph Debi Treloar/Vincent & Frieda Plasschaert's house in Brugge, Belgium; **56br** ph Debi Treloar/Catherine Chermayeff & Jonathan David's family home in New York, designed by Asfour Guzy Architects; **57a** ph Debi Treloar/family home, Bankside, London; **57b** ph Debi Treloar; **58al** ph Debi Treloar/a family home in Manhattan, designed by architect Amanda Martocchio and Gustavo Martinez Design; **58bl** ph Debi Treloar/The Swedish Chair – Lena Renkel Eriksson; **58r** Richard Hopkin's apartment in London designed by HM2; **58–59** ph Debi Treloar; **59ar** Catherine Chermayeff & Jonathan David's family home in New York designed by Asfour Guzy Architects; **59br** Simon Crookall's apartment in London designed by Urban Salon.

Architects and designers whose work is featured in this book

Alan Tanksley, Inc
+1 212 481 8456
Page 1.

Amanda Martocchio, Architect
189 Brushy Ridge Road
New Canaan, CT 06840
Page 58al.

**Annette Brederode and
Aleid Röntgen-Brederode**
Lijnbaansgracht 56d
1015 gs Amsterdam
Page 42l.

Asfour Guzy Architects
+1 212 334 9350
easfour@asfourguzy.com
Pages 56br, 59ar.

Azman Owens Architects
020 7739 8191
www.azmanowens.com
Pages 10r, 14bl.

Bowles and Linares
020 7229 9886
Page 17r.

Brookes Stacey Randall
020 7403 0707
www.bsr-architects.com
Pages 23ar, 31b, 37r.

Bruce Bierman Design, Inc.
+1 212 243 1935
www.biermandesign.com
Pages 52 main, 52–53.

Bruno Tanquerel
+33 1 43 57 03 93
Pages 9l, 21l, 29al, 44br, 46al.

Carden Cunietti
020 7229 8559
www.carden-cunietti.com
Pages 10l, 14ar, 33br.

Christopher Leach Design Ltd
07765 255566
mail@christopherleach.com
Page 23br.

Claire Bataille and Paul ibens
+32 3 231 3593
Fax: +32 3 213 8639
Pages 12–13, 13c.

Coburn Architecture
+1 718 875 5052
www.coburnarch.com
Page 49b.

Constanze von Unruh
020 8948 5533
www.constanzeinteriorprojects.com
Front jacket, page 21ar.

Coskun Fine Art London
020 7581 9056
www.coskunfineart.com
Page 22b.

David Khouri
Comma
+1 212 420 7866
www.comma-nyc.com
Pages 25, 51.

David Mikhail Architects
020 7377 8424
www.davidmikhail.com
Pages 9r, 19br, 33bl.

David Vanderhook
020 7729 3645
Pages 18r, 39r.

Dive Architects
020 7407 0955
www.divearchitects.com
Pages 40bl, 57a.

Garth Carter
Specialist interiors painter
07958 412953
Page 47br.

Gustavo Martinez Design
t.+ 1 212 686 3102
gmdecor@aol.com
Page 58al.

Heidi Wish
020 7737 7797
Pages 13r, 23al, 23bc, 28bl.

Helen Ellery
The Plot London
020 7251 8116
www.theplotlondon.com
Pages 45a both.

Hilton McConnico
+33 1 43 62 53 16
hmc@club-internet.fr
Page 41r.

HM2
020 7600 5151
andrew.hanson@harper-mackay.co.uk
Pages 22a, 24a, 58r.

Johanne Riss
+32 2 513 0900
www.johanneriss.com
Pages 32, 41l.

John Barman Inc.
+1 212 838 9443
www.johnbarman.com
Page 38a.

John Minshaw Designs Ltd
020 7258 0627
Page 16l.

Johnson Naylor
020 7490 8885
brian.johnson@johnsonnaylor.co.uk
Page 17c.

jwflowers.com
020 7735 7771
www.jwflowers.com
Page 54l.

Knott Architects
020 7263 8844
www.knottarchitects.co.uk
Pages 40r, 56l.

Kristiina Ratia Designs
+ 1 203 852 0027
Pages 46r, 47l & 47ar.

Littman Goddard Hogarth
020 7351 7871
www.lgh-architects.co.uk
Pages 8, 30br.

Marino + Giolito
+1 212 675 5737
marino.giolito@rcn.com
Pages 3, 14br, 24b, 33al.

Mark Kirkley
01424 812613
Page 29b.

Michael Nathenson
020 7431 6978
www.unique-environments.co.uk
Pages 19ar, 28br.

Moneo Brock Studio
+34 661 340 280
www.moneobrock.com
Pages 23ac, 38bl.

Mullman Seidman Architects
+ 1 212 431 0770
www.mullmanseidman.com
Pages 12l, 20l, 23bl, 26, 28a, 29ar,
37l, 50r, 52 inset, 54r.

Nigel Smith
020 7278 8802
n-smith@dircon.co.uk
Page 21br.

Orefelt Associates
020 7243 3181
orefelt@msn.com
Pages 20r, 31a, 40al, 44bl, 50l.

Paul Daly Design Studio Ltd
020 7613 4855
www.pauldaly.com
Page 53bl.

Reed Creative Services Ltd
020 7565 0066
Page 19l.

Roger Oates
Rugs and Runners Mail Order
Catalogue: 01531 631611
www.rogeroates.com
Page 15l.

Sally Storey
John Cullen Lighting
020 7371 5400
Page 19l.

Sandy Davidson Design
Fax: +1 320 659 2107
SandSandD@aol.com
Page 41c.

Sarah Featherstone
Featherstone Associates
020 7490 1212
www.featherstone-associates.co.uk
Pages 6–7.

Sera Hersham-Loftus
020 7286 5948
Pages 38br, 43r

Seth Stein Architects
020 8968 8581
www.sethstein.com
Page 30bl.

Sidnam Petrone Gartner Architects
+1 212 366 5500
www.spgarchitects.com
Page 18l.

Stephen Turvil Architects
020 7639 2212
turv@space1.demon.co.uk
Pages 30a, 48, 48–49.

Susan Cropper
www.63hlg.com
Page 2.

The Swedish Chair
020 8657 8560
www.theswedishchair.com
Page 58bl.

Tsao & McKown
+1 212 337 3800
Fax: +1 212 337 0013
Pages 34–35.

Urban Research Lab
020 8709 9060
www.urbanresearchlab.com
Pages 15r, 30–31a.

Urban Salon Architects
020 7357 8000
Pages 4r, 39l, 59br.

Vicente Wolf Associates, Inc.
+1 212 465 0590
Pages 11 both, 33ar.

VX design & architecture
ianchee@vxdesign.com
Page 36r.

William R. Hefner AIA
+1 323 931 1365
www.williamhefner.com
Page 41c.

ZG DESIGN
+1 631 329 7486
www.zgdesign.com
Page 14al.

index